ECHOES

for

grandma

with

my love

and devotion

ever

Contemporaries

EECCHHOOEESS

N.H. Pritchard

New York University Press
New York 1971

also by N.H. PRITCHARD

The Matrix: Poems 1960—1970
(Doubleday and Company)

CONTENTS

for
Sibella

for
Sibella

as
as
as
as
as
as
as
as
as
as
as
as
as
as
as
as
as bowers hour in the sun
as vying orbs make their pledge
as some heedy alter of the core taken leaf
as windy puddles predict the sun
as
as
as
as
as
as
as
as
as
as
as
as
as
as
as
as
as
as
as
as
as
as
as
as
as

as a
as a
as a
as a
as a
as a
as a
as a
as a
as a
as a
as a
as a
as a
as a
as a
as a
as a
as a
as a
as a
as a
as a
as a
as a
as a
as a
as a
as a
as a
as a
as a
as a
as a
as a
as a
as a half lulls
as a plane matched utmost by its wedge
as a
as a
as a
as a
as a

as a

as a   sneeze protruding on a field

as a

as a

as a

as a

as a

as a

as a

as a

as a

as a

as a

as a

as a

as a

as a

as a

as a

as a

as a

as a

as a

as a

as a

as a

as a

as a

as a

as a

as a

as a

as a

as a

as a

as a

as a

as a

as a

as a

as a

as a

as a

as a

as a

as a

as a

as a

as a

as a

as a

as a sedgy favour on its watch

as a veer vexed by a too

as a slightly regular become orange

as a

as a

as a

as a

as a

as a

as a

as a

as a

as a

as a

as a

as a

as a

as a

as a

as a

as a

as a

as a

as a

as a

as a

as a

as a

as a

as a

as a

as a

as a

as a

as a

as a

as a

as a

as a

as a

as a

as a

as a

as a

as a

as a

as a

as a

as a

as a

as a

as a

as a

as a

as a

as a

as a

as a

as a

as a

as a

as a

as a

as a

as a

as a

as a mooonless ooh boon

as a

as a moonless ooh boon

as a

as a

as a moonless ooh boon

as a moonless ooh boon

as a moonless ohh boon

as a

as a moonless ooh boon

as a

as a

as a

as a

as a

as a

as a

as a

as a

as a

as a

as a

as a

as a

as a

as a

as a

as a

as a

as a

as a

as a

as a

as a

as a

as a

as a

as a

as a

as a

as a

as a

as a

as a

as a

as a

as a

as a

as a

as a

as a

as a

as a

as a

as a

as a

as a

as a

as a

as a hoo

as a

as a

as a

as a

as a

as a

as a

as a

as a

as a

as a

as a

as a

as a

as a

as a

as a

as a

as a

as a

as a

as a

as a

as a

as a

as a hoo

as a hoo

as a hoo

as a hoo

as a hoo

as a hoo

as a hoo

as a hoo

as a

as a

as a

as a

as a

as a

as a

as a

as a

as a

as a

as a

as a hoo hooz

as a hoo hooz

as a

as a

as a hoo hooz

as a hoo hooz

as a

as a

as a hoo hooz

as a hoo hooz

as a

as a

as a hoo hooz

as a hoo hooz

as a

as a

as a hoo hooz

as a hoo hooz

as a

as a

as a hoo hooz

as a hoo hooz

as a

as a

as a hoo hooz

as a hoo hooz

as a

as a

as a hoo hooz

as a hoo hooz

as a

as a

as a hoo hooz

as a hoo hooz

as a

as a

as a hoo hooz

as a hoo hooz

as a

as a

as a hoo hooz

as a hoo hooz

as a hoo hooz
as a hoo hooz
as a hoo hooz
as a
as a
as a hoo hooz
as a hoo hooz
as a hoo hooz
as a hoo hooz
as a hoo hooz
as a
as a
as a hoo hooz
as a hoo hooz
as a hoo hooz
as a hoo hooz
as a hoo hooz
as a
as a
as a hoo hooz
as a hoo hooz
as a hoo hooz
as a hoo hooz
as a hoo hooz
as a
as a
as a hoo hooz
as a hoo hooz
as a hoo hooz
as a hoo hooz
as a hoo hooz
as a
as a
as a hoo hooz
as a hoo hooz
as a hoo hooz
as a hoo hooz
as a hoo hooz
as a
as a
as a hoo hooz
as a hoo hooz
as a hoo hooz
as a hoo hooz

as a
as a chipper brimming in a spout
as a
as a
as a
as a
as a
as a
as a
as a
as a
as a
as a
as a
as a
as a
as a
as a
as a
as a
as a
as a
as a
as a
as a
as a
as a
as a stubborn fray of toe
as a
as a fibrous livid in a mince
as a hazardous pluck flustered
as a
as a
as a
as a
as a
as a
as a
as a
as a felly hooz quell juices
as a
as a
as a

.d . u . s . t .

.m .a.w .o.f..w .a.n.i.n.g..w.r.u.n.g..t.h.e.i.r..l.i.k.e. .

.b.r.a.z.e.n..p.r.e.c.i.o.u.s..t.h.r.e.a.d.s..p.o.u.r.e.d. . .

.b.e.n.e.a.t.h..u.p.o.n..w.i.l.t..b.e.a.k.. .

.w.h.o.l.e..v.o.l.l.e.y..p.a.r.c.h.e.s.. . . . .

.s.t.a.r.c.h..m.e.a.t.s.. . . . .

.b.r.l.m..s.l.n.o.u.s....... . . . . .

.w.h.i.m.s..o.f..g.l.c.c.i.n.g..r.o.u.n.d. .

.c.r.o.o.k.e.d..d.r.a.u.g.t.h.y..c.r.a.w.l.s.. .

.d.e..e.p.c.o.w.e.r.s. . . . .

.t.a.t.t.e.r.e.d..a.n.d..s.t.i.t.c.h.e.d..b.o.n.e.s. .

.s.p.r.i.n.k.l.e.d..b.e.c.a.u.s.e. . . .

23

MINT

a r e o r d i d n ' t m i l k

s u r e l y s o m e o f i t s

b l u e w i l l b e r e s t i

n g s h o r t l y h u g e b a

l l o n s i n t h e m t o e s

THE WATCH

r are wat chth atre aps t hesum o fmir t h

a ll g row ingkno w n

& sim plybi r t h

di dspri ngit sda rken edli ghtt owea r

t h ehu mble omen o facar e

& istha the ightso r o und ofmi g h t

t h atfo rsom etim e

aft erwa r d s

t here

wer e

onl y

s mallso und s

FEAWE

perhaps that yawn should budge its lull

thrashing the rabid flinch

ashes of avid either

neither dull nor game

requested

several drank the fame

digested

few did gain

THE SHROUD

d imi sthepa stwit hits shro udo ff ear in g

ha ugh tyis t h ecas t

w it hit scrow dofglea r in gey e s

t h atca nn otse e

c ries t h ataha veno w hy

m ayb ebutpe bb lesbet weensa nda ndse a

junt

mool oio clish brodge

cence anis oio

mek mek isto plawe

WE NEED ---- please read this and see if you
qualify, if you do not care to take advantage of this
please pass it on to a friend.

grown on instead opens the door
a blind went away pulling
large numbers covered with rows
decidely

toward them some its own
dressed away with the rain
flying in borrowed kind
things in the basket

beside twisted ruddy before
without those mostly or an under
plundered nearly though feasted
delighted so as to be carried

arodnap

still

quarters

neither had them both

offerings of settlements

from such hence

out of the fire

in all sorts of

of calmly

to their own advantage

after a generous supper

carefully loosing the way

ownly

brought out the whole

swarming

carbon

eitwa heno heli sneat

lethe this taw

heta ubur heno heno

purte kanda gews

enab sapa het sas dasa

plint hethe tinga keet

odin ulte onga

dest chot hemo reeth

anem maga rom veroa

habi edin mest teep bove

dabas yot hedu

dindi ollo ollo tret

rovi ceda bogoe vean

hemu sofli oco stant

veco oode faske

stura aket pleg bafe

rilpe quage hiff

miftefe ipic tatek

noft oesmoe evon

ascem oco oco

oco

daffa

lesan

avin

egui

Tryingham
November
1970

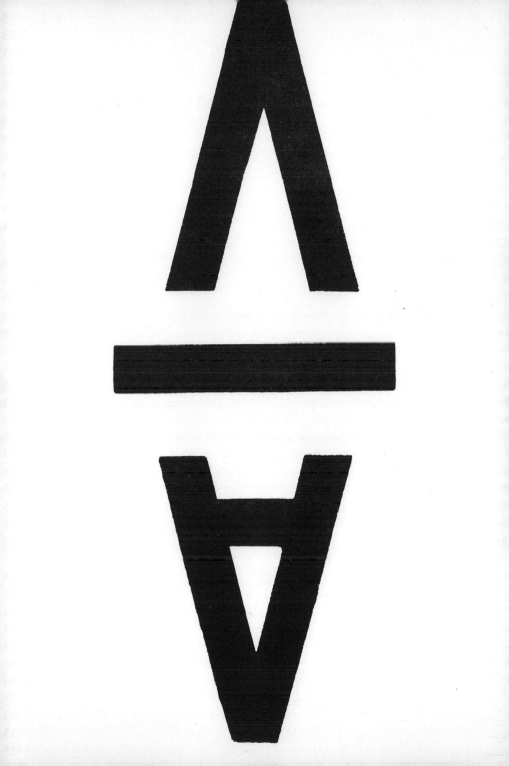

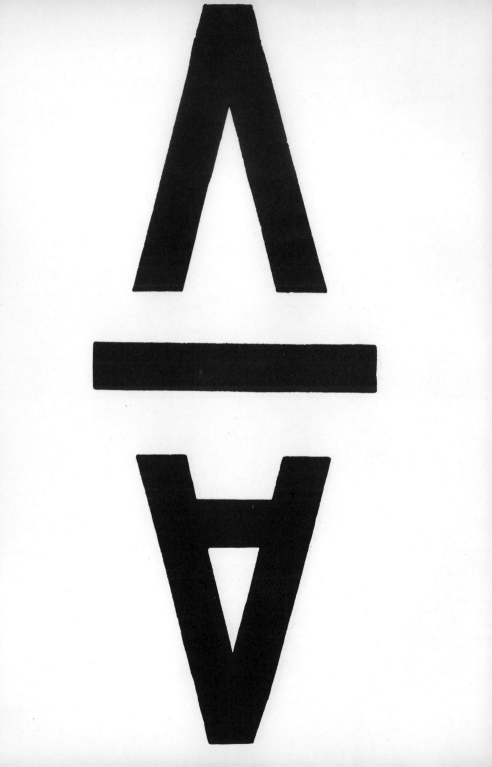

Glistening
Glistening
Glistening
Glistening
Glistening
Glistening
Glistening
Glistening
Glistening
Glistening Glistening Glistening Glistening Glistening Glistening
Glistening Glistening Glistening Glistening Glistening Glistening
Glistening Glistening Glistening Glistening Glistening Glistening

istening Glistening Glistening Glistening Glistening Glistening Glistening Glistening Gli
istening Glistening Glistening Glistening Glistening Glistening Glistening Glistening Gli
istening Glistening Glistening Glistening Glistening Glistening Glistening Glistening Gli

stening Glistening Glistening Glistening Glistening Glistening Glistening Glistening Gli
stening Glistening Glistening Glistening Glistening Glistening Glistening Glistening Gli
istening Glistening Glistening Glistening Glistening Glistening Glistening Glistening Gli

s blinks blinks blinks blinks blinks blinks blinks blinks blinks blinks blinks blinks blink
s blinks blinks blinks blinks blinks blinks blinks blinks blinks blinks blinks blinks blink
s blinks blinks blinks blinks blinks blinks blinks blinks blinks blinks blinks blinks blink

ıks blinks blinks blinks blinks blinks blinks blinks blinks blinks blinks blinks blinks blir
ıks blinks blinks blinks blinks blinks blinks blinks blinks blinks blinks blinks blinks blir
ıks blinks blinks blinks blinks blinks blinks blinks blinks blinks blinks blinks blinks blir

eht

ksud

ESCENDING
DESCENDING
DESCENDING
DESCENDING
DESCENDING
DESCENDING
DESCENDING
DESCENDING
DESCENDING
DESCENDING
DESCENDING
DESCENDING
DESCENDING
DESCENDING
ESCENDING
ESCENDING
ESCENDING
ESCENDING
ESCENDING
ESCENDING
ESCENDING
ESCENDING
ESCENDING
ESCENDING
ESCENDING
ESCENDING
ESCENDING
ESCENDING
ESCENDING
ESCENDING
ESCENDING
ESCENDING
ESCENDING
ESCENDING
ESCENDING
ESCENDING
ESCENDING
ESCENDING
SCENDING
SCENDING
SCENDING
SCENDING
SCENDING

ESCENDING
ESCENDING
ESCENDING
ESCENDING
ESCENDING
ESCENDING
ESCENDING
ESCENDING
ESCENDING
ESCENDING
ESCENDING
ESCENDING
ESCENDING
ESCENDING
ESCENDING
ESCENDING
ESCENDING
ESCENDING
ESCENDING
ESCENDING
ESCENDING
ESCENDING
ESCENDING
ESCENDING
ESCENDING
ESCENDING
ESCENDING
ESCENDING
ESCENDING
ESCENDING
ESCENDING
ESCENDING
ESCENDING
ESCENDING
ESCENDING
ESCENDING
ESCENDING
ESCENDING
ESCENDING
ESCENDING
ESCENDING
ESCENDING
SCENDING

f   oru   msofru   inedwi   ll

ing   echo   ing

  echo   echo

    ing   echo

         ing

  echo   ing echo

    echo

   ing

        echo

         ing

  ing

    echo

       echo

      ing

echo

       ing

     echo

  ing   echo

         ing

        ing

       echo

   echo

echo   ing

         ing

ing

  echo

      echo

    ing

  echo

echo   ing   ing

litsllits

litsllits

litsllits

litsllits

litsllits

litsllits

litsllits

litsllits

litsllits

litsllits

litsllits

litsllits

litsllits

litsllits

litsllits

litsllits

litsllits

litsllits

litsllits

litsllits

litsllits

litsllits

llits

llits

llits

llits

llitsllit

llitsllit

llitsllit

llitsllit

llitsllit

olliollivollivolliollivolliollivolliollivolliollivolliolliolliollirollirellirellirellirellirellitsllitsllitsllitsllitsllit

sllit

sllit

sllit

sllit

sllit

sllit

sllit

sllit

sllit

sllit

llitsllit

ark   eni   n

t hehus hof anci enthi ll

lou   dlyac   clai   ming   t   he   wan   e

l   i   keso   mestro   rmwi   thou   tanam   e

l   istles   sly   dim   in   is   hed   byase   a

p   roc   lai   ming   t   h   atem   pty

VIA
Rome — New york
1961-1970